TRUE UNDERSTANDING OF MAHATMA

TRUE UNDERSTANDING OF MAHATMA

JIGAR GIRISHBHAI PANDYA

This book will serve as a reference for old age people who are looking for salvation. Mahatma had once given freedom to the nation, but Mahatma has a strong action plan to give liberation as the next level of freedom. The only purpose of writing this as pictures and works defined in this book is that no one has ever shown in the past. This book is dedicated to the parents who gave birth to the same soul in this period of time as well.

The reason for Mahatma's rebirth is to complete the rest of the tasks prescribed by Lord Krishna and therefore he is still alive in front of all of you because of the blessings from the parents.

Contents

Preface	*vii*
Acknowledgements	*ix*
1. Prostrate	1
2. Reincarnation Of Mahatma	3
3. The Cause Of The Deluge	5
4. A Ray Of Light	7
5. Supreme Intelligence	9
6. Lord Of Yama	11
7. A Symbol Of Righteousness	13
8. A Symbol Of Liberation	14
9. Vibhasvan	16
10. The Ultimate Truth	18
11. Omniscient	21
12. King Of Planets	23
13. Symbol Of Supreme Wisdom	25
14. Cause Of Happiness	27
15. A Symbol Of Faith	29
16. Symbol Of The Great Physician	31
17. Mentor	33
List Of Past Births	35
Endorsments From The Celebrities	45
Thank You	55

Preface

Content Provides a complete and comprehensive overview of Lord Surya, the Sun God in Hinduism. It lists his many positive qualities and characteristics, portraying him as a powerful and benevolent deity who is revered and worshiped by Hindus. The language used in the content is rich and descriptive, reflecting the glory and importance of Lord Surya in Hindu belief. The content also includes references to various aspects of Hindu mythology and beliefs, such as the concept of Yuga and Lord Surya's role as the bestower of fruits of wisdom and karma. Overall, The content is presented in a clear and organized manner, making it easy to understand and follow. To improve the content, it would be helpful to provide more context on the role of Lord Surya in Hindu mythology and his importance in Hindu beliefs. This includes information about his origin, other May include their relationship with the gods and the legends and stories associated with them. Additionally, expanding on some of the specific qualities and characteristics mentioned in the material can provide a deeper understanding of Lord Surya and his importance in Hinduism. For example, more information can be provided about what it means for Lord Surya to be the conqueror of the universe or the source of the universe. It may also be helpful to provide some examples of anecdotes showing how Lord Surya is worshiped and worshiped, such as how he is depicted in Hindu art, how Hindus pray to him and perform rituals. or information about how they are celebrated in Hindu festivals. Adding some visual elements, such as images or illustrations, can also enhance the content. and easier to navigate. Finally, including information about the various interpretations or perspectives about Lord Surya in Hinduism further elaborates on his role and importance. A sharper and broader understanding can be gained. This book will help you understand the real meaning of life through the words of a single soul - Mahatma. Also, Mahatma has a strong plan to deliver 1000+ salvations ahead. Also Mahatma has also predicted the date of Mahapralaya. As everyone is searching for true purpose in life and this book will serve as a great reference for them. As we all have lost a loved one in the recent Corona times, they will feel relieved after seeing the real picture of the souls.

Acknowledgements

Please use Google Lens/Scanner to view this on your mobile.

CHAPTER ONE

Prostrate

I bow down to the Supreme Lord Surya/Swaminarayan (my brother who is the cause of all incarnations) who is the Vishwajith/conqueror of the universe, who performs a major function for the welfare of the universe, who is the soul of the universe, and who faces in all directions, that Visvesvara. is

He is the Lord of the Universe, He is the Source of the Universe, He is the Self-Controller who resides in the living beings as Prana, and He has complete control over the senses/ascetics, He represents the Yugas and the functions of the Yugas, He is dependent on Him.

Lord Shri Swaminarayan

CHAPTER TWO

Reincarnation of Mahatma

The cause of yuga and the end of yuga, He is the Mahayogi/Supreme Yogi who follows strict yogic practices, He is the symbol of supreme intelligence, He is the Mahatma who is very strong and powerful, He is mighty and all-pervasive, He is the Lord of all.

The Sun behind the face of "**Mahatma Gandhi**"

The same Mahatma is still alive; i.e. myself

He resides in Jivas as Atman/Soul, He is Lord of the Universe/ Bhuvaneshwar, He is compassionate towards Jivas, He symbolizes the destiny of Jivas, He is Bhutanatha who is the cause of origin.

Jeevas and He is the bestower of auspiciousness, He is the safest shelter of Jeevas, He is Kamalnath/who is the consort of Goddess Kamala, He is the symbol of joy and He is the bestower of happiness, He is the most desirable and the bestower of boons.

The worshiper who observes severe austerities, He gives bright rays to the universe, He is the source of Prana, He is the Supreme Lord who resides in the living beings as Prana, He is pleasant, beloved and loved by all, He is the epitome of wisdom.

Pagana, He is impressive with splendid earrings, He is flawless, He is mighty, He has supreme brilliance and Vayu as his army, He is steadfast, He is the giver of Mathi/Buddhi, He is Vidhata who scatters fruit.

Karma and bestows all kinds of auspiciousness to the worshiper, He is also a symbol of Kapardhi, Kalpa and Rudra, He is charming which is a symbol of Dharma, He is committed to renegade souls, He is not pliable to the wicked, His virtues are beyond description.

He is Maheshwar who is the Mahayogi, He is Aditya who is radiant who attracts the heart of the worshiper, He is self-restrained and serene, He is the epitome of passion and mercy, He awakens the lotus flowers with His bright rays, He is mounted on a chariot by seven horses.

CHAPTER THREE

The cause of the deluge

He is wonderful, He is faultless and very kind, He is the supreme medicine for living beings, Sanjivani, He is the Lord of living beings, He gives life to the entire universe, He is Jagathpati, He is invincible. They have the universe as their celestial abode, they are Vrishadhwaja which symbolizes virtue and radiance, they illuminate the entire universe with their supreme radiance.

I bow down to the Supreme Lord Surya/Swaminarayana who is Vrishakapi, He is Ravi who performs the works of imagination and also ends the Kalpa, He is seated on the one-wheeled wonderful chariot, He is the supreme ascetic who passes through the highest state.

Mahapralay

Supreme Consciousness, and He takes immense pleasure even in humorous play, He is divine, He is the Lord of the afflicted, He is Dhivaspati who is the Lord of Lords, He is the Lord of prowess, He accepts oblations from fire sacrifices.

He is Diwakar who has divine arms, He is the symbol of Yajna, He is the commander of Yajna, He represents sustenance, He is Svarnaretha who illuminates the universe with his powerful rays, He is Anshumali who appears as Para, Apara and Sthanarani/dispersed.

He is extremely influential, he is a symbol of insight, wisdom and knowledge, he is the sun, he is Prajapati, Savita, Vishnu and Anshuman, he is a safe haven for the worshiper, his powerful hands are infused with rich fragrance, he is determined.

That bright ray is unbearable, He is pathanga, pathaga, sthanu, vihanga, vihaga and the bestower of abundant boons to the worshiper, He is Haridhasva mounted on his celestial chariot drawn by the green colored Haryasva, He is the beloved of the universe.

He has three eyes., He is Sarvadamana who causes the deluge at the end of the ages, He resides as Prana in the living beings, He is the Bhishaka who cures diseases, He resides in the celestial abode, He is the protector of the three lokas, He is worshiped.

By the gods and all living beings, he is the symbol of Kaal, the Kalpana is the cause of the final deluge (strongly predicted that this age will end on **29-11-2025**) he is Vahni who symbolizes fire and austerity, he is Virochana whose supreme brightness Yes, it is opposite/different eye.

A ray of light

He has thousands of eyes, He is Purandhara, He has billions of powerful rays, He is clothed in many folds of the sky. And decked with various ornaments, He is the supreme deity, He is prayer, He is auspicious, He is a symbol of excellence in speech, wealth and eloquence.

An astral projection of the Mahatma's soul

He is the consort of Sripati/Goddess of wealth and resides in the house of wealth/Sriniketan. I bow down to the Supreme Lord Surya/ Swaminarayana who graciously accepts the sacrifices/devotional acts performed by the wise in holy shrines, is dear to his worshiper and appears before his ardent worshiper, is the epitome of fame and is the provider.

CHAPTER FIVE

Supreme Intelligence

He is the symbol of Supreme Intelligence, He is the Amarshrestha/Supreme God, He is Jishnu who is victorious, He is the Commander of the Universe, He represents the unfathomable ocean, He bestows wealth on his worshiper, He is the Dhatha that purifies the souls.

He is the Mandhata who removes all miseries, sorrows and insults/ defilements of his worshiper, he dispels the darkness of ignorance in his worshiper, he dispels the darkness, his bright rays resemble fire, he is the source of the essential element.

He remains extremely confidential, He is the animal worshiper who inspires faith with His powerful rays and He is the Lord of the living beings, the giver of wealth and well-being to living beings.

The one who showers the rays of light to the entire universe

He is Suresh who is worshiped by the gods, he is Aditya who is eternal and the object of desire, he is Ajita who is incomparable and bestows victory on his worshiper, he is invincible, he also appears movable and immovable.

He is the giver of happiness to the living, He is ever-willing, He is victorious and successful in all endeavors, He is personified as Parjanayogi, He acts as the preserver of life, He is supremely venerable, He is the purifier.

He is Pradhyodhana who has supreme effulgence, he is seated on a magnificent chariot, he illuminates the entire universe with his supreme effulgence, he is the samsara tharaka who sustains the living beings with his supreme effulgence, he is the mighty and supreme preceptor, he is the cause of the universe and beings, he is also the cause and effects, he is Marthanda and he is the commander of Marutha/the essential element air/breath/Lord of Marutha, he represents Marutha who has the ability to burn things that enter.

CHAPTER SIX

Lord of yama

He is the touch of fire, he symbolizes welfare, he is Lord of yama, he represents Varuna, he is Jagannath who has no desires/frustrations.

The king yama

He has beautiful eyes, He is Vivasavan and Hanuman, He represents cause and effect, He is the symbol of supreme brilliance, He is free to move at will, He represents fire, He ensures the existence of righteousness, He with his billions rays Illuminates the universe.

Of the bright rays, they are Sahastrashu, Divakara and Gabasthinemi who represent powerful rays of light, radiating intense luster, they are Sragvi who have innumerable wonderful rays.

I bow down to the Supreme Lord Surya/Swaminarayana who is Bhaskara who possesses supreme effulgence, who works for the welfare of the Suras, who is all-pervading, who is ardent and resplendent, who is Surpati and the Supreme Lord among the Gods, who is the Lord of Vachaspati/Speech.

He is Bhruhateja/He has intense luster and is Tejonidhi, He has Bhruhathakirthi/Infinite fame, He represents Bhruhspati/The preceptor of the gods, He has authentic vigor and is virtuous, He is not free from the shadow/eclipsing cast.

He is the bestower of infinite glories to his worshiper, he is the Mahavaidhya who cures all kinds of ailments with his powerful rays and is foremost in promoting welfare, he is worshiped by the folds and he is the leader of the folds, he has infinite glories.

He causes mental and physical suffering in the wicked and is able to rebuke the universe with his powerful rays, He has the luster of the precious yellow metal, He is rishikesh who has complete control over the senses, He is Padmanabha, He is the symbol of intense bliss.

CHAPTER SEVEN

A symbol of righteousness

He is Amukta who passes through eclipses, he is protected in wonderful armor, he is an orator/reciter, he is covered in armor and considers the universe as his abode, he has unconditional movement, he is the most glorious, he is the most secure for him. is a shelter.

The worshipper, he has faces in all directions, he penetrates all objects with his powerful rays, he is formed, he represents the flame of righteousness, he is affectionate to those who follow righteousness, he crushes the wicked like Lord Yama, he is the destroyer.

The worldly bond in the worshiper fulfills all the desires of his worshiper, He is Janesvara, He resides in the central part of Nabha/ Nakshatra, He is the absolute truth that permeates all objects, He is captivating and charming, He represents. He is worshiped by Hari, Har, Vayu, Ritu, Kaal and Anala/Agni as well as intellectuals.

He is Mahateja who has supreme brightness and dispels the darkness in the universe, He is praised by Mahendra, He is Prabhakara who is praised by holy hymns, He bestows life/longevity free from waste/anger, lust, greed, ego. . etc., all kinds of well-being, freedom from all kinds of diseases, happiness and all kinds of auspiciousness.

I bow to the Supreme Lord Swaminarayan who bestows good health, wonderful natural powers/achievement, wealth and prosperity/growth, good fortune and achievement in endeavours, He is Ahaspati who bestows valour, good health, intelligence, friends and family too. He is great, he is powerful, he is easily pleased, he is the symbol of righteousness and he executes and ensures righteous deeds, he is the bestower of splendor, he is loved by all.

CHAPTER EIGHT

A symbol of liberation

He penetrates the entire earth, He destroys the enemies, He is the symbol of true knowledge, He is the supreme knower and giver of knowledge, He is bright, He has thousands of bright rays, He performs the work of creation, He is endowed with majesty. Kayura who radiates intense radiance, represents fire, destroys the worldly bonds of devotees at his lotus feet, is worshiped with sacrificial fire, is the radiant supreme deity, illuminates all objects with his supreme radiance.

He is the symbol of auspiciousness, he is the bestower of auspiciousness to his worshiper, he represents the Kalpa and performs the Kalpana functions and regulates the rituals, he is the poet/wisdom, he performs all the auspicious works for the welfare of the living beings, he is personified. Kalpa, he is the recipient of all auspicious rites, he is fond of peace, he has pleasant nature, he is the symbol of peace and he is fond of peace, he does.

પુનરાવર્તિત જન્મોમાંથી આત્માઓને મુક્ત કરવાનું કાર્ય, તે છે. (આ આત્માના ફોટા છે જેને મુક્તિ મળી છે.)

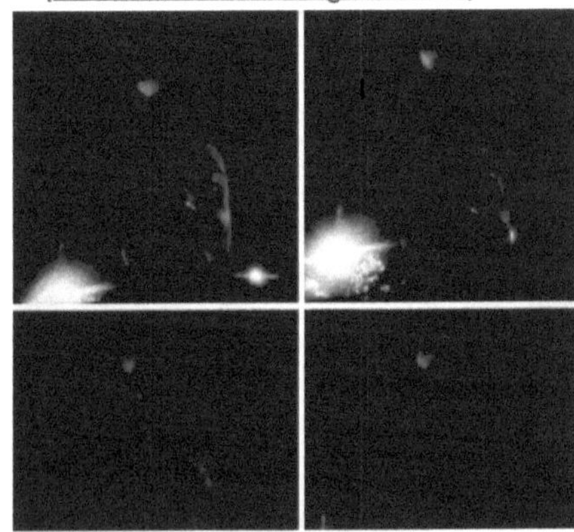

The task of releiving the souls from the past births in a form of salvation ; these are the real pictures of the soul who is achieiving the salvation.

Left: The spirit is being released from my head; Right side: The soul is freed and reaches the sky.

Suvarcha who has the highest luster. He is dominant/energetic. The three enliven the world and reside in the three. The world is dynamic and has supreme glory, it is power. Varna/Bhramana, Kshatriya, Vaishya and Shudra, he graciously accepts offerings from fire sacrifices, being foremost among them. The gods, he has supreme excellence, that is his essence. The Holy Vedas, it shines, remain as one of the essentials. Elements in nature, he explores the sky with the great. Speed, it is Khaga which symbolizes Shruti, it is Gopati/Krishna. He who is the Lord of Cows and Cowherds, is the Lord of Nine. The Lord of the planets and the galaxy, He is the protector of living beings and the prosperer of virility, He illuminates the entire universe with His radiance, He monitors the deeds of living beings, He undergoes yoga.

CHAPTER NINE

Vibhasvan

"He is Vibhasvan who destroys demons with the speed of wind, he protects his worshiper and removes all obstacles to them".

(અહી કોરોનાવાયરસ રોગોનું શ્રેષ્ઠ ઉદાહરણ છે જે એક દુષ્ટ રાક્ષસ સ્વરૂપ છે જે સમગ્ર વિશ્વમાં કોઈ જોઈ શક્તું નથી વિશ્વને બચાવવા મારા ભાઈ ભગવાન સ્વામિનારાયણે મને આ રાક્ષસને મારવામાં મદદ કરી)

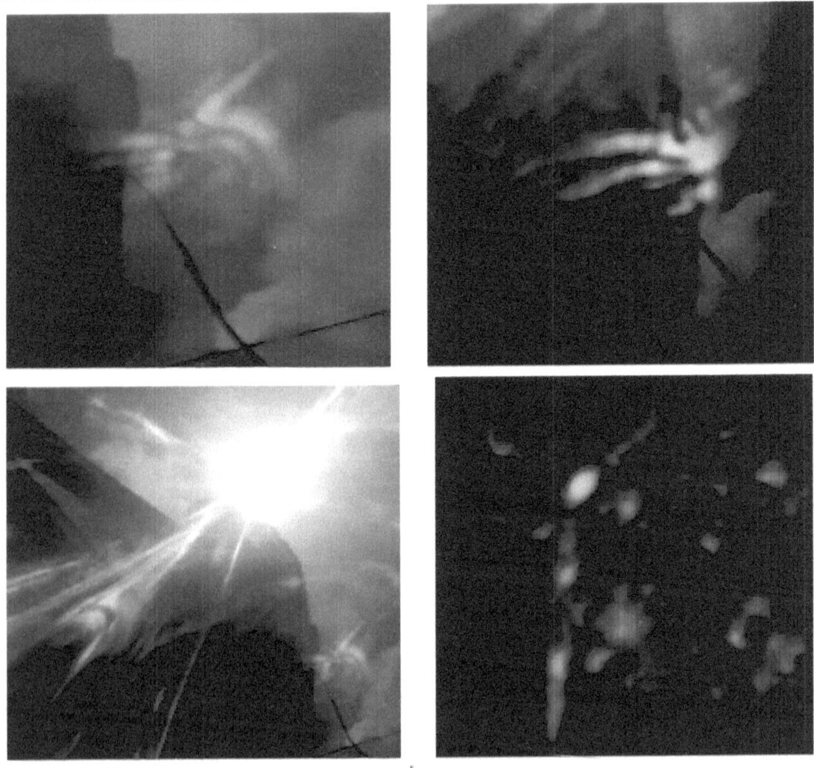

Here is the corona virus in the real form which is shown as two top pics and one below at left and the below one pic at right is jinns-jinnad (**in green**). Pictures of demons Green are all jinn and jinnat (they are not visible to any humans in the real world as per the quran)

He is adorned with a wonderful crown, he is charming and beautiful. I bow down to the Supreme Lord Surya/Swaminarayana Mariachi/ray of light, He is the symbol of knowledge, and he represents the field that works/ illuminates the universe with its vividness of Aditya, He is the symbol of virtue and strict discipline, auspiciousness, good With conduct he moves with intense devotion radiating light in all directions, he is the preceptor of beasts/birds/Anjaneya, the eagle, he moves forward in his own realm, he bestows praise and intelligence on the worshiper, he is clad in splendid white garments. He is praised by gods and sages, Brahmins sing His glories by reciting Samaveda, He is the giver of immense joy, He is praised by the Vedas, He is the essence of the Vedas.

CHAPTER TEN

The ultimate truth

He is Vedamurti, He is profound in the Chaturveda, He performs a major function by emitting radiant rays, He is invincible, He represents supreme bliss, He is the bestower of abundant boons to his worshiper, He takes austere vows and bestows. Capable of severe austerities, He is the closest associate of all living beings, He is adorned with various precious ornaments, He is the symbol of knowledge in scriptures and scriptures, He is the symbol of the syllable 'This', He is adorned with various precious ornaments. On His body, He worships Characterized, He is Chakrapani who is armed with Vajra weapons, He is dressed in wonderful clothes, He is loved and worshiped by the whole world.

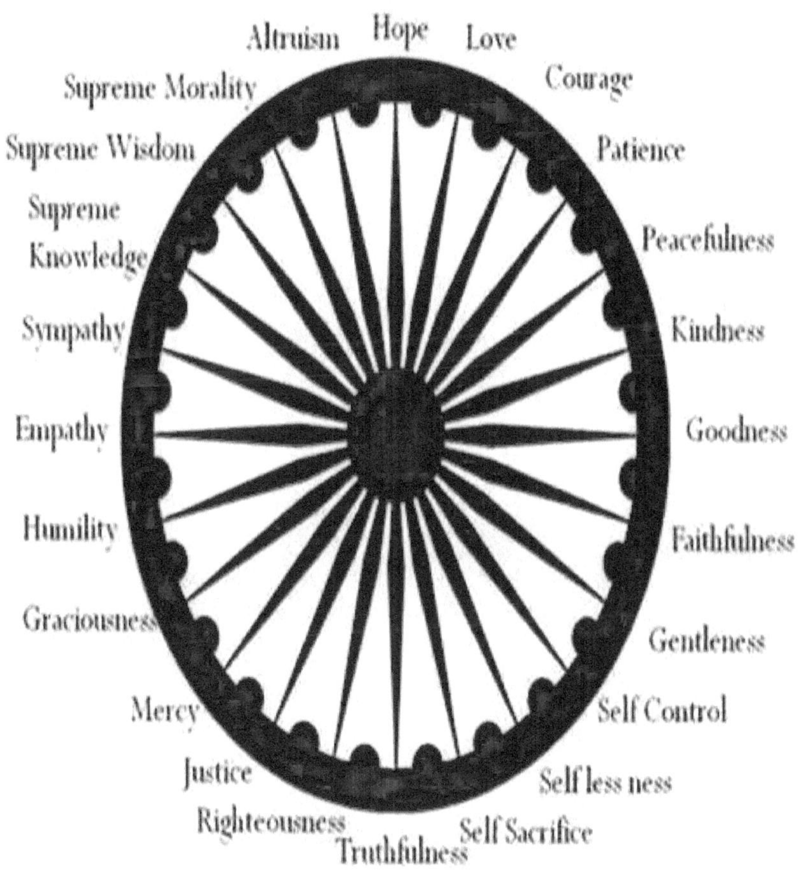

The symbol of Ultimate Truth - **24 Chakras**

He has powerful hands, He blossoms and diversifies nature with His bright rays, He represents virtue, He dispels darkness, He is the foremost who exists in all ages and causes change even in those ages, He is immeasurable. He is steeped in Yoga, He is God free from ego, He is the bestower of auspiciousness to His worshiper, He is the epitome of auspiciousness and flourishes the pious life engaged in virtuous deeds, He is the Supreme Truth. He is merciful and worthy of worship, he increases the happiness of his worshiper, his radiant rays are fresh representing youth, he is Hari who is youthful and powerful, the closest associate of his worshiper, he is sinless, It's lean. In blissful sleep, he is the lotus-born Lord Brahma, He is the Gana Lord, He represents the Samvathsara/Perennial/Varsha, He is the commander and cause of the movement of the Ruthu/Seasons and the Kalachakra/Samaya/Wheel of Time.

CHAPTER ELEVEN

Omniscient

I bow down to the imperishable Supreme Lord Surya/Swaminarayana, He who is born of illusion who is born of the lotus, He is the source of supreme radiance, He is divine, He is the symbol of supreme knowledge and benevolence, He is Soma and Govinda, He is Jagadhadhija. is primordial, has the color of precious yellow metal and is also dark, wears wonderful garments in the sky, is Hari who is beyond the senses, resides in living beings as prana, has various distinct forms, is SkandhaHe Para/ imperceptible, He is Puranjaya/Invincible, He is powerful and mighty, He is Bhaswana who is radiant, He is the bestower of salvation to His worshiper (see image below).

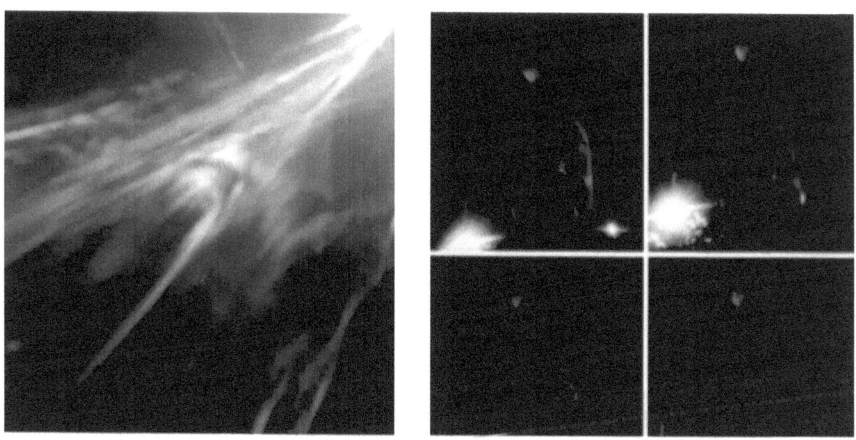

Real pictures of Salvation/Liberation

He has no birth, He is omniscient, He is Aditya who destroys the night horse and inauspiciousness in the worshiper's life, He is the cause of auspiciousness in the worshiper's life, He instantly destroys sins and evil in the worshiper, He is the symbol. Certain syllables, Mahamantra/Holy Mantras/Om are those. A manifestation of Visakha/Skandha, he is fond of display. Fire sacrifice, it represents Vishwakarma.

King of planets

He is Mahashakti/Supreme Force in the form of Dipti/Jyoti, He is Vihanga who has the luster of molten yellow metal, He is magnificent, He is famous like Indra, He destroys obstacles, He is compassionate, He is the father of Ashwinikumaras. He is the symbol of the Vedas, he has profound knowledge in the Vedas, he is omniscient. Prabhakara, Jitharipu, is the Aruna who has the bright rays and is. He is the benefactor, he is the charioteer, he represents Kubera, Skandha. That Mahita/Extremely Venerable, He is the King of the planets, He is the Lord. Of the planets, he resides in the galaxies in the assemblage of stars and the planets, he is Bhaskara who symbolizes eternal bliss, he represents valor, he crushed the pride of Mangal/Mars, he is the provider. All kinds of auspicious for his worshiper, he is impressive. And pure, it is the bestower of auspiciousness and can repel it. Similarly, it represents good deeds and discipline. It dries up at the time of absorption.

King of Planets - Sun

He represents religious vows and practices, he is a staunch follower of austerities, he is chaturmukha/charmukhi, he is garlanded with lotus flower, he resides in living beings as soul, he is spotless and dispassionate, he is absolute truth, he is. Unsullied by qualities like sattvik, rajas and tamas, he is a storehouse of qualities, he is faultless, he is pundarikaksha whose eyes are like the petals of a lotus flower, he is easily attainable, he is absorbed in yogic practice.

I bow down to the Supreme Lord Surya/Swaminarayana who has innumerable radiant rays, He is the Lord of the seasons, He is all-pervading, He symbolizes intelligence, wisdom, clarity of speech and reliability, He represents auspiciousness, He is garlanded with flowers, He is supreme. Tej, He is dear to Hari, He represents illusion, He is alert/attentive, resolute and imperishable, He is Prabhu/Shaktiman who represents Anala/Agni and Pawan, He is energetic and mighty, He is the Supreme Lord, He is luxurious.

CHAPTER THIRTEEN

Symbol of Supreme Wisdom

He is Purusha and flawless among Purushas/Purushottama, He is the Lord of Vidyadharas, He is the epitome of supreme wisdom and fortune, He is divine with incomparable qualities, He is Sriman/symbol of wealth, He is personified as the universe, He represents fortune and Auspiciousness, he is a symbol of prosperity, he is kind, his bright rays are able to provide freedom from repeated births.

 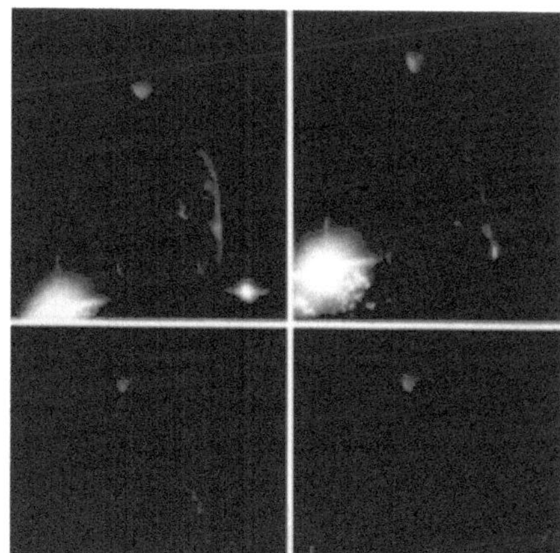

Freedom from the repeated births

He is also dispassionate and passionate, he has a bright appearance, he is benevolent, he has a subtle form, he has a calm nature, he ensures prosperity and habitable places, he is Bhuthara who is personified as the Lord of Earth and Earth. , that is. He is innocent and has three eyes, he is personified as a Mahavaraha/wild boar, he is the purifier of souls, he works for the welfare of the universe and its beings, he is evident as the deluge at the end of the age which causes intense fear. He represents Chaturveda/ Riga, Yajur, Sama and Atharva, He is wide-awake, He is eternal, He has various forms,

He is Chakravarti/He who moves forward without any hindrance, He is compassionate, He is Mahesvara, He Sitting on one. Magnificent Chariot, He is Yekaki, He is seated on a wonderful chariot driven by seven horses, He is Parathapara/Supreme Lord, He is Primordial, He is fixed in orbit and traverses vast distances, He is spotless, He is Pushkar, He has excellent is a ray of light. He is the favorite of Vasava/in. He is the Lord of Indra and Vasu, He is the Lord of Vasuman and Vasu, He is the symbol of the Lord of Fire, He is Vasupradha/He is the provider of bright rays of light, He is powerful,.

He is the symbol of supreme wisdom and knowledge and the sacred hymns, He represents the chief . He is the symbol of the Lord of Fire, He is Vasupradha/ He is the provider of bright rays of light, He is powerful, He is the symbol of supreme wisdom and knowledge and the sacred hymns, He represents the main deity of solemn vows during the observance of any ritual, He is the Lord of the poor. and it protects the victims.

CHAPTER FOURTEEN

Cause of happiness

It is the reason for all. I will bow to the Supreme Lord Surya/ Swaminarayana who represents one of the nine divine treasures of God. Kubera/Neelkanth, He is the Lord of Wealth, He symbolizes the Chaturveda, He speaks joyfully.

He is Vasatkara who performs fire sacrifices and oblations, he is the performer of fire. The sacrifice, by which he sanctifies the sacrificial fire with offerings by reciting 'svaha', he is Janardana who is the cause of happiness, he is Narayana who sits in the milky ocean. is the form of In male/human form, his luminous body like molten metal passes through the eclipse, he represents Vayu, he is worshiped by Sura and Asura, he represents the ornament in the galaxy, he is pure, he is the unsullied place, he is faultless. /The root is light, He is illustrious, He radiates intense luster, His intense luster penetrates the entire universe, He is omniscient, He is the bestower of abundant boons on worship, He is the epitome of righteousness, He is the cause of illusion.

He is the brother of Vishnubhatta/Lord Vishnu/Lord Swaminarayan.

Lord Swaminarayan / Vishnubhatra

He is Eternal, He is very kind like Savitri/Mother.

He is the ruler of the living beings and the universe, He is the most famous deity, He is Virata/Tejaswi with a distinctive mark on his neck, He is Saptarachi/Agni, His magnificent chariot is driven by seven horses, He is worshiped in the Sapta Lokas/ 7 realms of the universe. is It is Jagannath who is the symbol of wealth and prosperity, He is charming with supreme effulgence, He resides in all beings as Atman/Soul, He is accessible, He is the cause of the universe and its life.

It is dear to the seventh/lunar day of the fortnight. It is a symbol of prosperity. It is Madhava who is spotless. It symbolizes wisdom and knowledge. He is Madhusudhana who is the slayer of the demon Madhu. He is/is descended from the Angira clan. Angira, he is the comet/ball of fire which constantly orbits as the source of life, he is the delighter and the giver of happiness to the living beings, he is the supreme ascetic who bestows welfare by his intense luster, he is the cause of suffering. He is the Lord of the well-behaved, with his intense heat causing the misery of the wicked.

CHAPTER FIFTEEN

A symbol of faith

His brilliance is impossible to fathom, He is amiable to the virtuous, He has a pleasing disposition, His glorious chariot moves through the clouds, He is the Lord of the universe and its creatures, He is the Jagathapita/ Father of the Universe who is pleased. He is Sharva the cause of sorrow, He dwells the most secret in the middle of the clouds, He is omnipresent, He is the cause of the happiness of the universe, He is the leader of the universe and the destroyer of the enemies of Sur, He is the symbol of faith. He is the bestower of auspiciousness and wealth, he is worshipable as the supreme deity, he is faultless, therefore he is the chief deity. I bow down to the Supreme Lord Swaminarayan, He circles the highest Mount Meru with the stars and planets, He protects Mount Mahameru which is the abode of Lord Brahma and the Deities, He is Dharanidhara, He is embodied in the form of the Universe, He is the King of Truth. It affirms the existence of righteousness and wickedness.

He is Rathadhyaksha/Supreme Lord seated on a magnificent chariot, He is Rathpati seated on a wonderful chariot, He is stable and represents Anala/Agni/Wind, He is strong, He is thapi/source of heat, He is God. Among the stars, he is praised by virtuous people, he is the symbol of pious work, he is the giver of devotion to those who are devoted to him, he is Swarbhanu/Krishna, he is Vihaga, he is the best deity, he is excellent. He plays a major role in the functioning of the universe, he is the destroyer of all kinds of diseases, he is the provider of well-being.

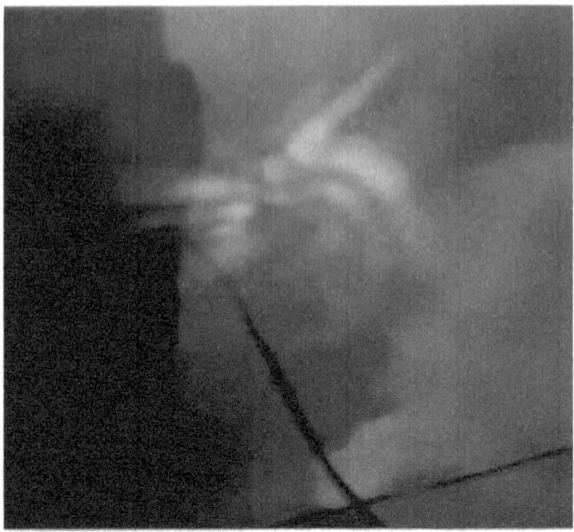

Corona disease in monstrous form

He is brave and invincible, he is Yekanatha, he sits on a wonderful chariot driven by seven horses. He is the father of Shanaischar. He is Vaivaswath who is a staunch follower of righteousness and takes great vows. Garnished with a garland of various fresh attractive flowers, it is the anala that moves constantly and radiates intense luster in all directions.

He represents valor and he bestows virtuous offspring for the worshipper, he is the symbol of sacred hymns and he is powerful, he is superior and he is dear to Shambhu. He is Ishwareshwar who is the Lord of pious and virtuous people. Virtuous people, it makes countless distinctions in the path of life and eradicates souls from the bonds of repeated births.

CHAPTER SIXTEEN

Symbol of the Great Physician

He guides us to cross the ocean of samsara safely, He represents Agni who has seven tongues, He has thousands of bright rays, He is the charioteer who is invincible, He is generous, He is the symbol of righteousness and He gives righteousness to His worshiper. is a provider. He is the Loksakshi who is awake, He is the Lokguru/Guru of the universe, He is the Lord of the universe. It carries the moon as a celestial vehicle. He represents the subtle form of air, he holds the divine bow in his hand and is an expert in the use of the bow, he carries a pinnac and a bow, he is very enthusiastic, he is not free from illusion, his imagination eventually becomes unpleasant, he An excellent, powerful and supreme deity, he is armed with various powerful weapons. He represents supreme wisdom and knowledge, he is Lohithanga who has attractive limbs that have the luster of precious yellow metal, he is unattainable for the deprived, he is the destroyer of enemies.

I bow down to the Supreme Lord Surya/Swaminarayana who is Eternal, He is the Bestower of virtues to His worshiper, He is always steeped in righteousness, He is Trivikrama, He is Nilalohita who resides in the center of the three sacred letters, which are blue in color. He is also Savita and Samitanjaya/Ajay.

He is profound in the knowledge of the Vedas, He wields the divine bow in Sharanga, He has a colossal form, He destroys enemies with evil weapons, He works for the welfare of the universe and its creatures, He is the Supreme Lord who radiates intense lustre. In the whole universe, he is the protector of the sky, he is Dhrivaspati, he is eloquent, he represents Vasuki, he is the symbol of the great physician, he is the descendant of Atri, he is mighty, he is Dvadashathama, he spreads happiness in the lives of people. He observes the strict austerities of bhramacarya and discipline, he is bright, he is adorned with a wonderful crown, he is an amshuman who holds a lotus flower in his hand, he has a joyful disposition, he is adorned with a garland of lotus flowers, he has divine.

He shines in the evening, He is impressive and incomparable, He is a mighty warrior/Maharath, He is seated on a magnificent chariot, He is the Supreme Lord who is beyond the triple gunas, He is untainted by Sattva, Rajas and Tamasic qualities, He destroys errors. is He gives the final judgment immediately, after considering the matter thoroughly, He is the symbol of innocence and supreme intelligence, He is incomparable, He undergoes eclipses, He is the bestower of wealth, salvation and abundant devotion to the worshiper, He is. The lord of the planets who removes all the evil effects caused by the motion of the planets, he is charming, he is spotless, he is very attractive, he represents one of the seven tongues of fire, he is magnificent, he radiates intense luster. He is the good commander, he is the lover of musical notes, he is the symbol of divination, he removes the bad effects caused by the planets.

CHAPTER SEVENTEEN

Mentor

He is composed, He destroys the enemies of the gods, He bestows abundant devotion on His worshiper, He has four hands, He is the supreme ascetic, He is the Lord of yogis. I bow to the Supreme Lord Surya/Swaminarayana who has innumerable forms, possesses the supreme luster of a precious jewel, illuminates the entire universe with his effulgence, resides in the vast expanse of the solar system, mounts the wondrous chariot with one wheel. . Magnificently seated on a golden chariot, He has the luster of a precious yellow metal, He needs no support, He fervently searches the sky, He is the authority of righteousness and karma of living beings, He is the witness of the righteous deeds of pious people.

It is eternal, it is worshiped by sages and rishis, it shines with brilliant colors at dusk, it is a symbol of achievement, it is worshiped by Goddess Sandhya.

He is pleased to grant kingdoms to His worshiper, He takes immense pleasure by means of atonement, He destroys the miseries of His ardent devotees, He guides safely to cross the ocean of samsara, He is the Supreme Lord who removes all kinds of fears of His worshiper.

Delighted in bestowing a kingdom on his worshiper, He takes immense pleasure by means of propitiation, He destroys the miseries of His ardent devotees, He guides safely to cross the ocean of worlds, He is the Supreme Lord who removes all kinds of fear of His worshiper. He cannot be seen by the senses, He has immense prowess, He is Lord of Manu and Lord of Manvantara.

List Of Past Births

This was all about the knowledge of Mahatma but now we will discuss all the previous births of Mahatma as well depicted as below :

1. <u>King Solomon (Son of King David)</u> (Read more: https://en.wikipedia.org/wiki/Solomon)

King Solomon

2. King Lakshmana (Lord Rama's brother) (Read more: https://en.wikipedia.org/wiki/Lakshmana)

King Lakshman

3. Balarama (Brother of Lord Krishna) (Read more : https://en.wikipedia.org/wiki/Balarama)

Balaram

4.   Arjuna/Partha   (Mahabharata)   (Read   more:
https://en.wikipedia.org/wiki/Arjuna)

Arjuna - Krishna

5. Chhatrapati Shivaji King(Read more : Search it on Google.)

The King Shivaji

6. Sant Sri Gopalanand Swami (Read more: https://en.wikipedia.org/wiki/Gopalanand_Swami)

Goplanand Swami

7. Sant Sri Tulsidas (Read more: https://en.wikipedia.org/wiki/Tulsidas)

Tulasidas

8. Saint Sri Ramanuja (Read more: https://en.wikipedia.org/wiki/Ramanuja)

Ramanujacharya

9. Mahatma Gandhi (Read more: https://en.wikipedia.org/wiki/ Mahatma_Gandhi)

Mahatma Gandhi

10. Hazrat Sulaiman (Prophet in Islam) (Read more: https://en.wikipedia.org/wiki/Solomon)

Hazrat Suleman

11. Jigar Pandya (Author himself) (Yet to be listed on Wikipedia)

Jigar Pandya - Author

Endorsments From The Celebrities

Enter Caption

Enter Caption

Enter Caption

Enter Caption

Enter Caption

Enter Caption

Enter Caption

Enter Caption

Enter Caption

Enter Caption

Thank You

Thank You